The
RAINBOW
is for Yahuah

Written by Brittani Ramirez

Printed in The United States of America

WHY DO WE USE "YAH" & "YHWH"?

In our books, we call God "Yah" because it's a special way to say
His Name. Did you know "God" is more like a title than His actual
Name? It's like calling your dad "Dad"
instead of using his real name!
In Hebrew, God's Name is written with four special letters:

YOD, HEY, VAV, HEY

In English, we write these letters as YHWH.
Some people pronounce His Name as "Yahuah," but a shorter,
beautiful way to say it is "Yah." In fact, every time you say
"HalleluYah," you're saying "Praise Yah!" How amazing is that?
We hope you enjoy this adventure, feel brave and loved, and
remember that Yah is guiding you every step of the way!

The rainbow is for **Yahuah**, a promise so grand,
Stretching across the sky, painted by His hand.
In vibrant hues, it shines so bright,
A symbol of His love, pure and light.

Long ago, in days of old,
Yahuah's people faced a world untold.
The flood came down, the waters raged,
But through it all, **Yah's** love engaged.

In Bereshit,
the story unfolds,
Noach and the ark,
a tale retold.

When the rain stopped
and skies turned blue,
A Keshet (Rainbow) appeared,
Yahuah's promise was true.

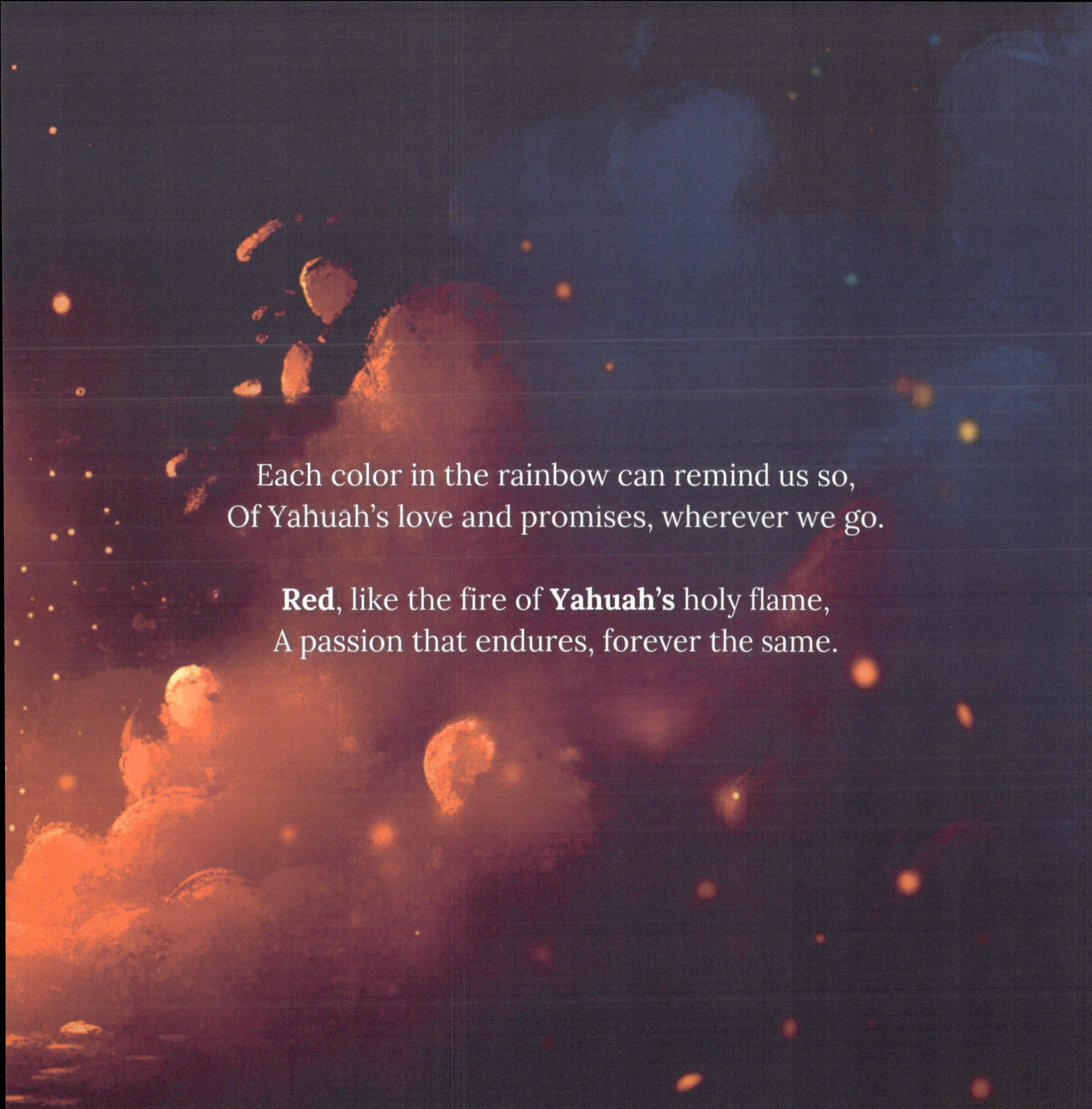
Each color in the rainbow can remind us so,
Of Yahuah's love and promises, wherever we go.

Red, like the fire of Yahuah's holy flame,
A passion that endures, forever the same.

Orange, like the warmth of the rising sun,
A new day beginning, **Yahuah's** will being done.

and **Yellow** beams bright, a golden ray,
Guiding us through trials, lighting our way.

Green like the fields, where life springs anew,
A reminder of **Yahuah's** provision, faithful and true.

Blue as the heavens, vast and serene,
A reflection of **Yahuah's** peace, steady and keen.

Indigo whispers of wisdom so deep,
A call to seek knowledge and promises to keep.

Violet, soft as a flower's bloom,
A reminder of **Yahuah's** grace,
dispelling all gloom.

Together they shine, a divine array,
Pointing to **Yahuah's** faithfulness every day.

The rainbow's seven, a covenant sign,
Yahuah's love and faithfulness, forever divine.
In its beauty, His promises glow,
A constant reminder wherever we go.

In Ezekiel's vision, **Yahuah's** glory was shown,
Encircled by a rainbow, a heavenly throne.

In Revelation, the promise appears,
A rainbow of hope, wiping away tears.

Through every storm, **Yahuah's** light will stay,
Guiding His children, showing the way.

So look to the sky when the rain is through,
And see **Yahuah's** covenant, painted anew.

The rainbow's arc,
so vivid and wide,
Is Yah's promise of love
by our side.

In every color, in every hue,
Yahuah's faithfulness
shines, steady and true.

For the rainbow is for **Yahuah**, a gift from above,
A symbol of His promises and **unending love**.

May this story bring
joy and delight,
A reminder of **Yah's** love,
shining so bright.

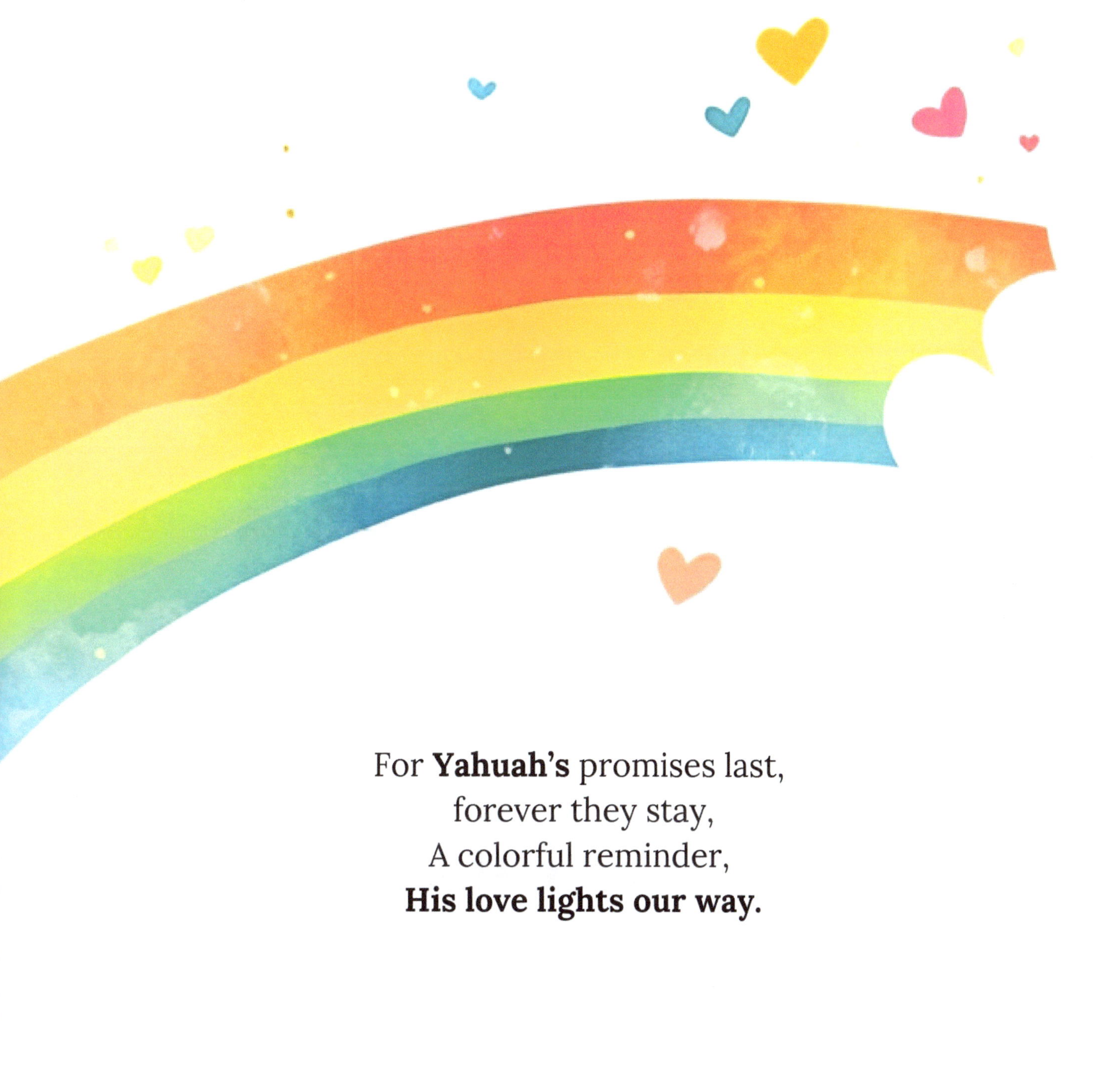

For **Yahuah's** promises last,
forever they stay,
A colorful reminder,
His love lights our way.

SCRIPTURE REFERENCES

GENESIS 9:13-16

"I set My rainbow in the cloud, and it shall be for the sign of the covenant between Me and the earth. It shall be, when I bring a cloud over the earth, that the rainbow shall be seen in the cloud; and I will remember My covenant which is between Me and you and every living creature of all flesh; the waters shall never again become a flood to destroy all flesh."

EZEKIEL 1:28

"Like the appearance of a rainbow in a cloud on a rainy day, so was the appearance of the brightness all around it. This was the appearance of the likeness of the glory of YHWH."

REVELATION 4:3

"And He who sat there was like a jasper and a sardius stone in appearance; and there was a rainbow around the throne, in appearance like an emerald."

GLOSSARY OF HEBREW TERMS

Bereshit
(bə·reh·SHEET)

Genesis in English
The first book of the Torah/ Bible, meaning "In the Beginning.

Noach
(NO-akh)

Noah in English
The righteous man chosen by YHWH to build the ark and preserve life during the flood.

YHWH
(Yah-oo-ah)

Yahuah
The sacred and personal name of the Creator, representing His eternal, unchanging nature and covenant faithfulness.

Brit
(BREET)

Covenant in English
A sacred promise or agreement made by YHWH, such as His covenant with Noach symbolized by the rainbow.

Keshet
(KEH-shet)

Rainbow in English
A sign of YHWH's covenant with all living creatures after the flood.

Shamayim
(Sha-MAH-yeem)

Heavens in English
The skies or the heavenly realm where YHWH's glory is revealed.

Eretz
(EH-retz)

Earth in English
The land or the world created by YHWH.

Mabul
(mah-BOOL)

Flood in English
The great flood sent by YHWH during the days of Noach to cleanse the earth.

Torah
(TOH-rah)

TheLaw/ Instruction
The first five books of the Bible, often referred to as "the teachings" or "instructions" of YHWH

Looking for more books like this?

Looking for more books like this? Visit our website at www.scribblesandscriptures.com to explore more!

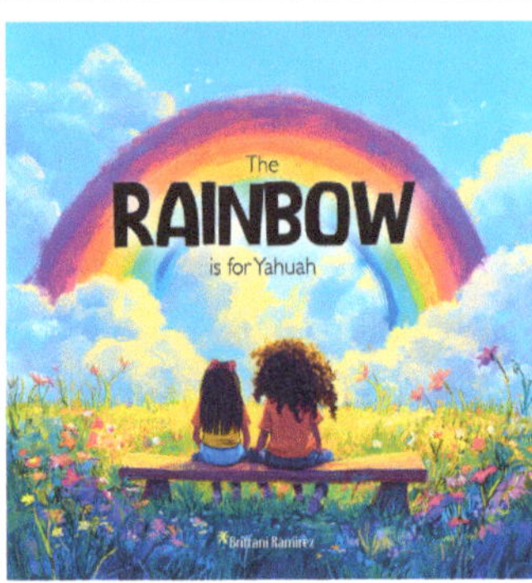

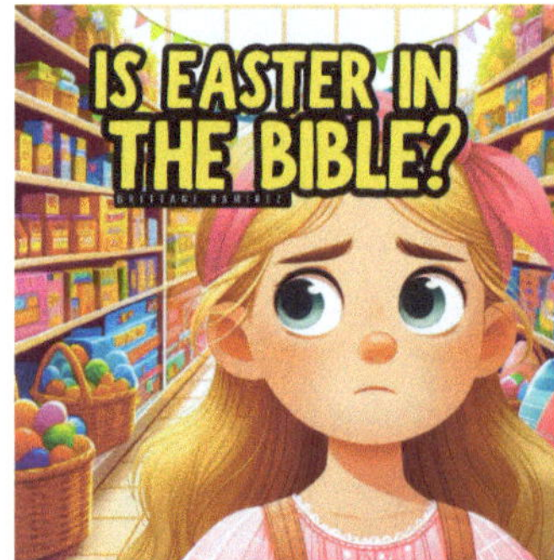

Love Our Books? Join Scribbles Book Club!

If you want all our books but don't want to buy them all at once, Scribbles Book Club is perfect for you! Get a new book delivered straight to your door every month, along with fun extras like stickers and bookmarks. Scan the QR code to start your monthly adventure today!